OUR SOLAR SYSTEM
PLUTO AND OTHER DWARF PLANETS
SMALL OBJECTS AROUND THE SUN

by Mari Schuh

pogo

Ideas for Parents and Teachers

Pogo Books let children practice reading informational text while introducing them to nonfiction features such as headings, labels, sidebars, maps, and diagrams, as well as a table of contents, glossary, and index.

Carefully leveled text with a strong photo match offers early fluent readers the support they need to succeed.

Before Reading

- "Walk" through the book and point out the various nonfiction features. Ask the student what purpose each feature serves.

- Look at the glossary together. Read and discuss the words.

Read the Book

- Have the child read the book independently.

- Invite him or her to list questions that arise from reading.

After Reading

- Discuss the child's questions. Talk about how he or she might find answers to those questions.

- Prompt the child to think more. Ask: How are Pluto and other dwarf planets different than planets? How are they the same?

Pogo Books are published by Jump!
5357 Penn Avenue South
Minneapolis, MN 55419
www.jumplibrary.com

Library of Congress Cataloging-in-Publication Data is available at www.loc.gov or upon request from the publisher.

ISBN: 979-8-88524-364-3 (hardcover)
ISBN: 979-8-88524-365-0 (paperback)
ISBN: 979-8-88524-366-7 (ebook)

Editor: Jenna Gleisner
Designer: Emma Bersie

Photo Credits: Shutterstock, cover (background), cover (top left), cover (top right), cover (bottom left), cover (bottom right); iStock, cover (top middle), 3 (right); 24K-Production/iStock, 1; Ianm35/iStock, 3 (left); NASA/Southwest Research Institute/Alex Parker, 4; NASA/ESA/STScI, 5; MR.Somchat Parkaythong/Shutterstock, 6-7 (Sun); Artsiom P/Shutterstock, 6-7 (Pluto); Pike-28/Shutterstock, 8 (Sun); NASA images/Shutterstock, 8 (Pluto); Wow Galaxy/Shutterstock, 9 (Pluto); thebull/Shutterstock, 9 (background); NASA/Johns Hopkins University Applied Physics Laboratory/Southwest Research Institute, 10-11, 12-13 (Charon); Claudio Caridi/Shutterstock, 12-13 (Pluto); somov ivan/Shutterstock, 12-13 (background), 15 (background); Think_About_Life/Shutterstock, 14 (Eris), 23 (right); Maliflower73/Shutterstock, 14 (background); ManuMata/Shutterstock, 15 (Makemake); Diego Barucco/Shutterstock, 16-17; NASA/JPL-Caltech/UCLA/MPS/DLR/IDA, 18-19; Dragon Images/Shutterstock, 20-21; mrgao/iStock, 23 (left).

Printed in the United States of America at Corporate Graphics in North Mankato, Minnesota.

For Jake, Angela, and Paige

TABLE OF CONTENTS

Haumea

Eris

CHAPTER 1

WHAT IS A DWARF PLANET?

An **astronomer** discovered Pluto with a **telescope** in 1930. For a long time, Pluto was considered a **planet**. Scientists thought of planets as big objects in the **solar system**. Pluto was the smallest planet. It was the farthest from the Sun.

Sun

Pluto

In the 1990s, scientists discovered many small, icy objects near Pluto. These also **orbit** the Sun. In 2005, scientists discovered an object about the same size as Pluto. They started thinking differently about what makes an object a planet.

In 2006, a group of astronomers made a big change. The group said planets have a clear path. As they orbit the Sun, they do not share their space with other big objects. Planets are also round or nearly round.

The group also identified **dwarf planets**. Like planets, they orbit the Sun. They are round or nearly round. But dwarf planets are smaller. They are not big enough to keep objects away. They share their orbit with other objects. Pluto was now a dwarf planet.

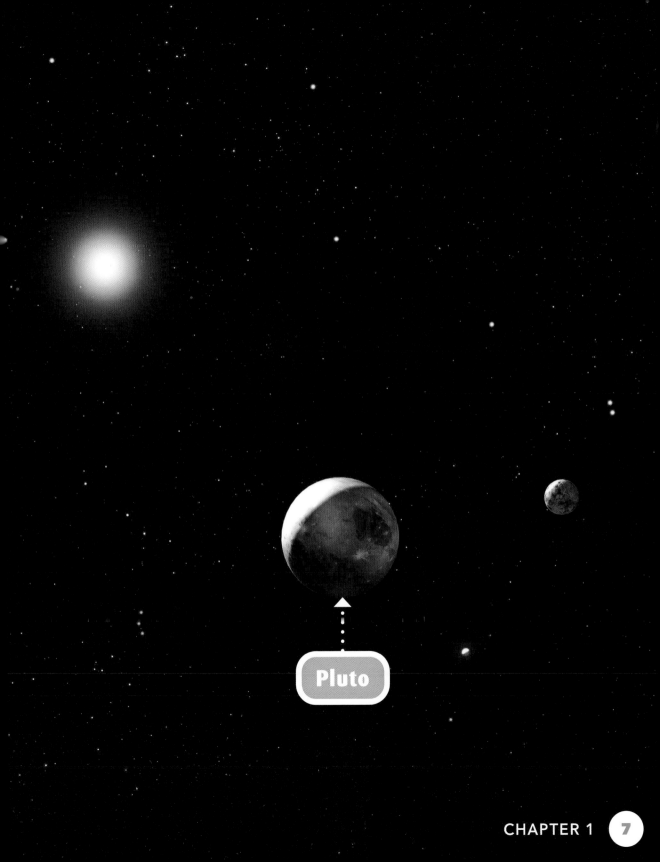

Pluto

CHAPTER 2

ALL ABOUT PLUTO

Planets orbit the Sun in a circular path. Pluto's orbit is different. Its path has an oval shape. It also tilts.

Pluto's orbit

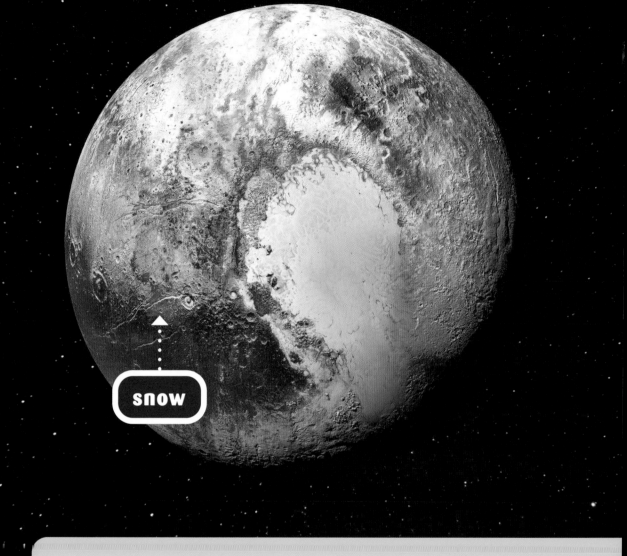

snow

Pluto has a thin **atmosphere**. Ice on its surface changes. How? It turns to gas when Pluto is close to the Sun. When Pluto is far from the Sun, it snows. The snow is red!

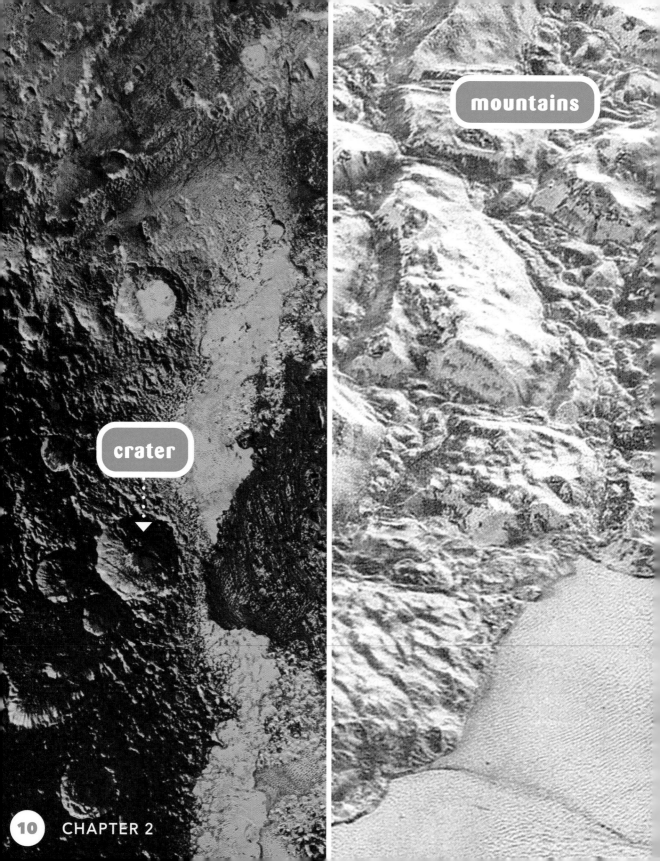

mountains

crater

Craters and plains cover Pluto's surface. There are also mountains and valleys. The mountains are made of ice. Some are covered with frozen gas!

DID YOU KNOW?

In 2015, the *New Horizons* **spacecraft** made history. It visited Pluto. It took the first close-up photos.

Pluto has five moons. They are Charon, Hydra, Kerberos, Nix, and Styx. Charon is the biggest. It is about half as wide as Pluto.

Charon

CHAPTER 3

....

OTHER DWARF PLANETS

As of 2022, there are five official dwarf planets. Eris is the farthest from the Sun. One trip around the Sun takes Eris 557 Earth years! It takes sunlight more than nine hours to reach Eris.

Eris

Makemake is cold and icy. The ice **reflects** a lot of sunlight. This makes Makemake very bright.

Makemake

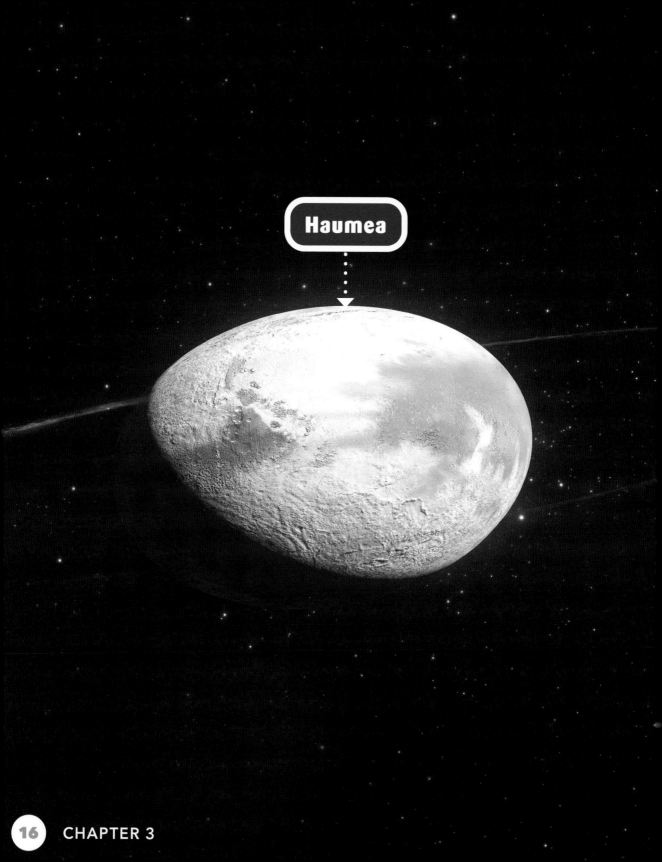

Haumea

All planets and dwarf planets spin. One full spin is one day. Haumea spins quickly. It has one of the fastest spins in the solar system. One spin, or day, on Haumea is only four hours!

DID YOU KNOW?

Haumea is shaped like an egg. Why? It spins so fast its shape changed!

Ceres is in the inner solar system. Its surface is rocky and dusty. It has a lot of salt. Why? Scientists think Ceres has salt water inside it. Some water might have come to the surface. It **evaporated**. It left salt behind.

Ceres

Where are dwarf planets in the solar system? Take a look!

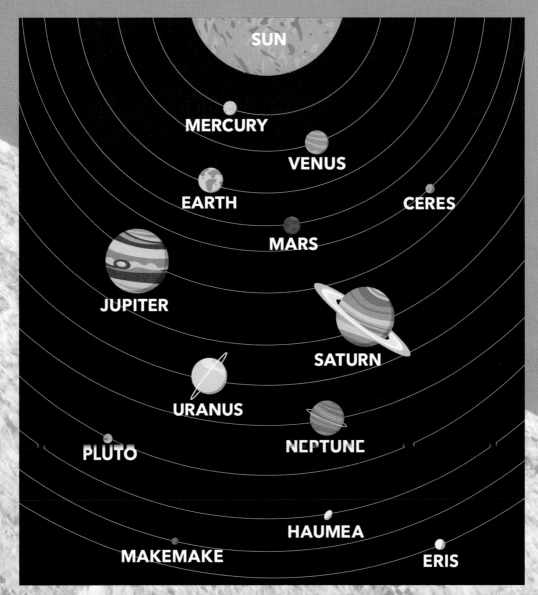

There could be more than 100 dwarf planets. Scientists want to find them! They continue to discover more objects in space.

If you discovered a dwarf planet, what would you name it? Why?

DID YOU KNOW?

Scientists know that Ceres has water under its surface. It might have more water than Earth! Living things need water to live. Scientists want to look for signs of life on Ceres.

ACTIVITIES & TOOLS

TRY THIS!

COMPARING PLANET SIZES

Dwarf planets are smaller than planets. See how their sizes compare in this fun activity!

What You Need:
- basketball
- volleyball
- softball
- baseball
- raspberry
- blueberry
- two nickels
- two corn kernels
- mustard seed
- sesame seed
- poppy seed

1. Gather round items from around your home, classroom, or school that will stand for the eight planets in our solar system.

2. Look back at the diagram in the book. Place your items in the order the planets are from the Sun. Start with the item you chose for Mercury. This planet is closest to the Sun.

3. Now gather much smaller items, such as corn kernels and seeds, to stand for the dwarf planets.

4. Look back at the diagram again. Place the dwarf planets between or around the planets, in the order they are from the Sun.

5. Study your planets. How do the sizes of the dwarf planets compare to the planets? Do you think the size of the dwarf planets makes it easier or harder for scientists to study them? Why?

astronomer: A scientist who studies stars, planets, and space.

atmosphere: The mixture of gases that surrounds a planet.

craters: Large holes in the ground that are made when pieces of rock or metal in space crash into a planet or moon.

dwarf planets: Objects that orbit the Sun but do not have a clear path.

evaporated: Changed from a liquid to a gas.

orbit: To travel in a circular path around something.

planet: A large body that orbits, or travels in circles around, the Sun.

reflects: Throws back light, heat, or sound from a surface.

solar system: The Sun, together with its orbiting bodies, such as the planets, their moons, and asteroids, comets, and meteors.

spacecraft: A vehicle that travels in space.

telescope: A device that uses lenses or mirrors in a long tube to make faraway objects appear bigger and closer.

Ceres

Makemake

INDEX

TO LEARN MORE

Finding more information is as easy as 1, 2, 3.

1. **Go to www.factsurfer.com**
2. **Enter "Plutoandotherdwarfplanets" into the search box.**
3. **Choose your book to see a list of websites.**

FACT SURFER